Catholic
PRAYERS

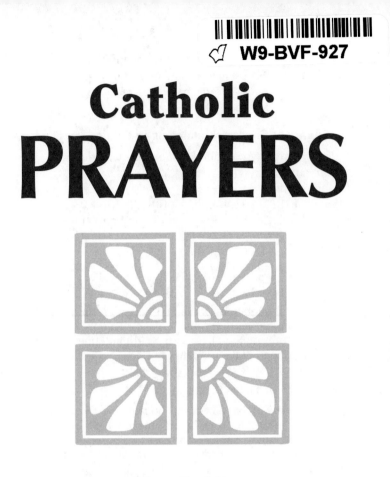

Compiled by
Sean M. David Mayer, FSP

Pauline
BOOKS & MEDIA

Boston

Nihil Obstat:: Rev. Msgr. Dennis F. Sheehan, STD
Imprimatur: ✠ Most Rev. Richard G. Lennon
Apostolic Admin. for the Archdiocese of Boston
March 5, 2003

Library of Congress Cataloging-in-Publication Data

Catholic prayers / compiled by Sean M. David Mayer.
  p. cm.
Includes index.
  ISBN 0-8198-1562-4 (pbk.) — 0-8198-1564-0
  1. Catholic Church—Prayer-books and devotions—
English. I. Mayer, Sean M. David.
  BX1981 .C36 2003
  242'.802—dc21

                                    2003001219

Cover design by Helen Rita Lane, FSP

Printed and published in the U.S.A. by Pauline Books & Media, 50 Saint Paul's Avenue, Boston, MA 02130-3491.

www.pauline.org

Pauline Books & Media is the publishing house of the Daughters of St. Paul, an international congregation of women religious serving the Church with the communications media.

1 2 3 4 5 6 7 8 9   11 10 09 08 07 06 05 04 03

Contents

The Sign of the Cross

In the name of the Father, and of the Son, and of the Holy Spirit. Amen.

The Lord's Prayer

Our Father, who art in heaven, hallowed be thy name; thy kingdom come; thy will be done on earth as it is in heaven. Give us this day our daily bread, forgive us our trespasses, as we forgive those who trespass against us, lead us not into temptation, but deliver us from evil. Amen.

Hail Mary

Hail Mary, full of grace! The Lord is with you. Blessed are you among women, and blessed is the fruit of your womb, Jesus. Holy Mary, Mother of God, pray for us sinners, now and at the hour of our death. Amen.

Glory Be

Glory to the Father, and to the Son, and to the Holy Spirit. As it was in the beginning, is now, and will be for ever. Amen.

Morning Offering

Divine Heart of Jesus, through the Immaculate Heart of Mary, I offer you all my prayers, works, joys, and sufferings of this day, in reparation for sins, and for the salvation of all men and women, according to the special intentions of the Pope, in the grace of the Holy Spirit, for the glory of the heavenly Father. Amen.

An Evening Prayer

I adore you, my God, and I love you with all my heart. I thank you for having created me, made me a Christian, and kept me this day. Forgive me for whatever evil I have done today, and accept my good intentions and actions. Take care of me while I sleep and deliver me from all danger. May your grace be always with me and with all my loved ones. Amen.

An Act of Faith

O my God, I firmly believe that you are one God in three divine Persons, Father, Son, and Holy Spirit; I believe that your divine Son became man and died for our sins, and that he will come to judge the living and the dead. I believe these and all the truths which the holy Catholic Church teaches, because you have revealed them, who can neither deceive nor be deceived.

An Act of Hope

O my God, relying on your infinite goodness and promises, I hope to obtain pardon of my sins, the help of your grace, and life everlasting through the merits of Jesus Christ, my Lord and Redeemer.

An Act of Love

O my God, I love you above all things, with my whole heart and soul, because you are all-good and worthy of all love. I love my neighbor as myself for the love of you. I forgive all who have injured me, and I ask pardon of all whom I have injured.

Abide with Me

Abide with me; fast falls the eventide;
The darkness deepens;
  Lord with me abide;

When other helpers fail,
  and comforts flee,
Help of the helpless,
  O abide with me.

Swift to its close ebbs out
  life's little day;
Earth's joys grow dim,
  its glories pass away;
Change and decay in all around I see;
O thou who changest not,
  abide with me.

Hold thou thy Cross
  before my closing eyes;
Shine through the gloom,
  and point me to the skies;
Heaven's morning breaks,
  and earth's vain shadows flee;
In life, in death, O Lord,
  abide with me.

H. F. Lyte

Prayer for the Gift of Sleep

Lord, gift me with swift sleep,
the gentle quiet of dream-filled rest.
Now, this tiresome day behind,
send your Spirit to calm a weary mind.
All hours are blessed by the Lord,
all hours blessed by you,
grant me a few more tomorrows to do
  your will. Amen.

Fr. Joe Coleman

The Apostles' Creed

I believe in God, the Father almighty,
creator of heaven and earth. I believe
in Jesus Christ, his only Son, our Lord.
He was conceived by the power of the
Holy Spirit and born of the Virgin Mary.
He suffered under Pontius Pilate, was
crucified, died, and was buried. He de-
scended to the dead. On the third day
he arose again. He ascended into heav-

en, and is seated at the right hand of the Father. He will come again to judge the living and the dead. I believe in the Holy Spirit, the holy Catholic Church, the communion of saints, the forgiveness of sins, the resurrection of the body, and life everlasting. Amen.

When We Most Need You

When all feels dark
and hope is hard to find,
remind us, loving God,
that you are closest to us
at the points where we most need you.
For nothing,
nothing at all,
can take us away from your love
in Christ Jesus. Amen.

Angela Ashwin

Prayer of Trust in Darkness

O Lord God,
I am in a barren land,
parched and cracked by the violence
of the north wind and the cold.
But as you see,
I believe in you.
You will send me both dew and
  warmth
when I am ready.

St. Jane Frances de Chantal

Psalm 63
Longing for God

O God, you are my God, I seek you,
  my soul thirsts for you;
my flesh faints for you,
  as in a dry and weary land where
    there is no water.

So I have looked upon you in the
    sanctuary,
  beholding your power and glory.
Because your steadfast love is better
    than life,
  my lips will praise you.
So I will bless you as long as I live;
  I will lift up my hands and call on
    your name.

My soul is satisfied as with a rich
    feast,
  and my mouth praises you with
    joyful lips
when I think of you on my bed,
  and meditate on you in the watches
    of the night;
for you have been my help,
  and in the shadows of your wings
    I sing for joy.
My soul clings to you;
  your right hand upholds me.

Let Nothing Disturb Thee

Let nothing disturb thee,
nothing affright thee;
all things are passing;
God never changeth;
patient endurance
attaineth to all things;
who God possesseth
in nothing is wanting;
alone God sufficeth.

St. Teresa of Avila

Too Late
Have I Loved You

Too late have I loved you, O Beauty
so ancient and so new, too late have I
loved you! Behold, you were within me,
while I was outside: it was there that I
sought you, and, a deformed creature,
rushed headlong upon these things of

beauty which you have made. You were with me, but I was not with you. They kept me far from you, those fair things which, if they were not in you, would not exist at all. You have called to me, and have cried out, and have shattered my deafness. You have blazed forth with light, and have shone upon me, and you have put my blindness to flight! You have sent forth fragrance, and I have drawn in my breath, and I pant after you. I have tasted you, and I hunger and thirst after you. You have touched me, and I have burned for your peace.

St. Augustine (Confessions, Book X, 27)

We Adore You, Jesus Truth

Jesus, Divine Master, we adore you as the Word Incarnate sent by the Father to teach us life-giving truths. You are uncreated Truth, the only Master. You alone have words of eternal life. We thank you for having gifted us with the light of reason and faith, and for having called us to the light of glory in heaven. We believe in you and the teachings of the Church, and we pray that your Word may enlighten our minds. Master, show us the treasures of your wisdom; let us know the Father; make us your true disciples. Increase our faith so that we may reach eternal life in heaven.

Blessed James Alberione

We Adore You, Jesus Way

Jesus, Divine Master, we adore you as the Beloved of the Father, the sole Way to him. We thank you because you showed us how to live a holy life, making yourself our model. We contemplate you throughout your earthly life. You have invited us to follow your example. We want to follow your teachings, treating everyone with love and respect. Draw us to yourself, so that by following in your footsteps and practicing self-sacrifice, we may seek only your will. Increase hope in us and the desire to be similar to you, so that we may rejoice to hear your words: "Come…inherit the kingdom prepared for you from the foundation of the world…. Just as you did it to one of the least of these,…you did it to me" (Mt 25:34, 40).

Blessed James Alberione

We Adore You, Jesus, Living in the Church

Jesus, Divine Master, we adore you living in the Church, the Mystical Body of Christ, through which you bring us to eternal life. We thank you for having joined us together as members of the Church, in which you continue to be for humanity the Way, the Truth, and the Life. We ask that those who do not believe may receive the gift of faith, that those who are separated may be brought into full communion, and that all people may be united in faith, in a common hope, in charity. Assist the Church and its leaders; sustain the People of God. Lord Jesus, our wish is yours: that there may be one fold under one Shepherd, so that we may all be together in heaven.

Blessed James Alberione

Prayer of Longing for Christ

Come, true light.

Come, life eternal.

Come, hidden mystery.

Come, treasure without name.

Come, reality beyond all words.

Come, person beyond all
  understanding.

Come, rejoicing without end.

Come, light that knows no evening.

Come, raising up of the fallen.

Come, resurrection of the dead.

From a tenth-century prayer to Christ

Hymn to Christ

Christ of our sufferings,
Christ of our sacrifices,
Christ of our Gethsemane,
Christ of our difficult
 transformations,
Christ of our faithful service
 to our neighbor,
Christ of our pilgrimage,
Christ of our community,
Christ our Redeemer,
Christ our Brother! Amen.

Pope John Paul II

Prayer Before a Crucifix

Behold, my beloved and good Jesus, I cast myself upon my knees in your sight, and with the most fervent desire of my soul I pray and beseech you to impress upon my heart lively sentiments of faith, hope, and love, with true repentance for my sins and a most firm desire of amendment; while with deep affection and grief of soul I consider within myself and contemplate your five most precious wounds, having before my eyes that which David, the prophet, long ago spoke about you, my Jesus:

"They have pierced my hands and my feet; I can count all my bones" (Ps 22:17–18).

Stations of the Cross

O merciful Jesus! With a contrite heart and penitent spirit, I undertake this devotion of the Way of the Cross in honor of your bitter sufferings and death.

I give humble thanks for the boundless love which impelled you to carry the cross and to die for my redemption.

The following is said before each station:

R. We adore you, O Christ, and we bless you.

V. Because by your holy cross you have redeemed the world!

A brief period of silent meditation is observed at each station:

✝ **FIRST STATION**
Jesus Before Pilate

He was silent.

✝ **SECOND STATION**
Jesus Is Laden with the Cross

He was resigned.

✝ **THIRD STATION**
Jesus Falls under the Weight of the Cross

He was exhausted.

✝ **FOURTH STATION**
Jesus Meets His Blessed Mother

He was sorrowful.

✝ **FIFTH STATION**
Simon of Cyrene Helps Jesus to Carry His Cross

He was vulnerable.

✝ **SIXTH STATION**
Veronica Wipes the Face of Jesus

He was grateful.

✝ SEVENTH STATION
Jesus Falls the Second Time

He was destitute.

✝ EIGHTH STATION
**Jesus Consoles the
Women of Jerusalem**

He was compassionate.

✝ NINTH STATION
Jesus Falls the Third Time

He was crushed.

✝ TENTH STATION
Jesus Is Stripped of His Garments

He was lonely.

✝ ELEVENTH STATION
Jesus Is Nailed to the Cross

He was slain.

✝ TWELFTH STATION
Jesus Dies on the Cross

He was faithful.

✟ **THIRTEENTH STATION**
Jesus Is Taken Down from the Cross

He was helpless.

✟ **FOURTEENTH STATION**
Jesus Is Laid in the Tomb

He was at rest.

On the third day he rose again!

CLOSING PRAYER

Lord, look upon your family. For our sake our Lord Jesus Christ unhesitatingly suffered betrayal and underwent the torment of the cross. By meditating on his passion grant me the grace to accept my own sufferings and unite them to his sacrifice. I ask this in Jesus' name. Amen.

Canticle from St. Paul's Letter to the Philippians

Let the same mind be in you that was
  in Christ Jesus,
who, though he was in the form
    of God,
  did not regard equality with God
  as something to be exploited,
but emptied himself,
  taking the form of a slave,
  being born in human likeness.
And being found in human form,
  he humbled himself
  and became obedient
    to the point of death:
  even death on a cross.

Therefore God also
    highly exalted him
  and gave him the name
  that is above every name,

so that at the name of Jesus
  every knee should bend,
  in heaven and on earth and under
    the earth,
and every tongue should confess
  that Jesus Christ is Lord,
  to the glory of God the Father.

Phil. 2:5–11

In Thanksgiving

O Jesus, eternal God, thank You for Your countless graces and blessings. Let every beat of my heart be a new hymn of thanksgiving to You, O God. Let every drop of my blood circulate for You, Lord. My soul is one hymn in adoration of Your mercy. I love You, God, for Yourself alone.

St. Faustina Kowalska (1794)

Live in Us, Jesus

Jesus, Divine Master, we adore you with the angels who sang the reasons for your Incarnation: glory to God and peace to all people. We thank you for having called us to share in your saving mission. Enkindle in us your flame of love for God and for all humanity. Live in us so that we may radiate you through our prayer, suffering, and work, as well as by word, example, and deed. Send good laborers into your harvest. Enlighten preachers, teachers, and writers; infuse in them the Holy Spirit and the Spirit's seven gifts. Come, Master and Lord! Teach and reign, through Mary, Mother, Teacher, and Queen.

Blessed James Alberione

Soul of Christ

Soul of Christ, sanctify me.
Body of Christ, save me.
Blood of Christ, inebriate me.
Water from the side of Christ,
  wash me.
O good Jesus, hear me.
Within your wounds hide me.
Permit me not to be separated
  from you.
From the evil enemy
  defend me.
In the hour of my death call me.
And bid me come to you,
that with your saints I my praise you
for ever and ever. Amen.

Conversation with Jesus Master after Receiving the Eucharist

I adore you present in me, Incarnate Word, only-begotten Son and splendor of the Father, born of Mary. I thank you, sole Master and Truth, for coming to me. With Mary I offer you to the Father: through you, with you, in you, may there be eternal praise, thanksgiving, and petition for peace for all people. Enlighten my mind; make me a faithful disciple of the Church; make mine a life of faith. Give me an understanding of the Scriptures; make me your enthusiastic apostle. Let the light of your Gospel shine to the ends of the earth.

Jesus, you are the Way I want to follow; the perfect model to imitate. I want my whole life to be configured to you.

You were humble and obedient: make me similar to you.

You loved unselfishly and with a pure heart: make me similar to you.

You were poor in spirit and patient: make me similar to you.

You loved everyone and sought to bring everyone to your Father: make me similar to you.

O Jesus, my life, my joy, and source of all good, I love you. May I more generously love you and the people you came to save.

You are the vine and I am the branch; I want to remain united to you always so as to bear much fruit.

You are the fount: pour out an ever greater abundance of grace to sanctify me.

You are my head, I, your member: communicate to me your Holy Spirit with the Spirit's gifts; may your kingdom come through Mary.

Console and save all my dear ones. Bring those who have died into your presence. Assist all who share your mission of spreading the Good News. Bless the Church with many vocations to the priesthood and religious life.

Blessed James Alberione

O Sacred Banquet

O Sacred Banquet,
in which we receive Christ;
we remember his passion;
we are filled with grace,
and we are given a pledge of future
  glory, alleluia!

St. Thomas Aquinas

Prayer of Presence

Lord, we come before you
  here in the Eucharist,
and we believe
  that you are looking at us
  and listening to our prayers.
You are so great and so holy,
  we adore you.
You have given us everything,
  we thank you.
We have sinned against you,
  and we ask your pardon
  with hearts full of sorrow.
You are rich in mercy;
  we ask you to grant us all the graces
  which will help us draw closer to
  you.

Traditional, adapted

We Adore You Hidden God

We adore you, hidden God,
  in this Sacrament—
Christ our Savior and our King,
  truly present.
Humbly we come before you,
  hearts completely won,
lost in wonder at the great marvels
  you have done.
Sense alone will fail to grasp
  this great mystery.
Faith and love enable our
  human eyes to see.
We believe all the truth
  that God's own Son has shown.
Nothing can be truer than
  what he has made known.
On the cross was hidden your divinity.
Hidden here before us, too,
  is your humanity.
We in faith profess them both,
  one in our belief.

And we make our own the plea
  of the dying thief.
Thomas saw your wounds,
  O Lord; these we do not see.
Yet do we confess you
  Lord and God to be.
May this faith of ours ever grow
  and our hope increase.
May our burning love for you,
  Jesus, never cease.
O most blest memorial
  of Christ's sacrifice,
giver of eternal life—
  Bread of paradise!
You are food for our hung'ring souls;
  live in us, O Lord.
Be the only goal we seek;
  be our sole reward.
We are cleansed, Lord, by your blood;
  filled with grace and love.
One drop shed to save the world
  would have been enough.

Yet you suffered and died for us,
  mankind lost in sin.
O how great a price you paid
  to redemption win.
Jesus, whom we now behold
  veiled from human sight,
grant us what we thirst for so:
  that one day we might
face to face behold your vision,
  bliss you have in store,
love surpassing space and time,
  joy forevermore.

St. Thomas Aquinas
(Translated by Daughters of St. Paul)

Prayer for the Gifts of the Holy Spirit

Divine Holy Spirit, eternal love of the
  Father and of the Son,
I adore you, I thank you, I love you
  and I ask your forgiveness for all

the times I have sinned against you
and against my neighbor.

Descend with many graces
on those ordained as bishops and
  priests,
on those consecrated as men and
  women religious,
on those who receive the Sacrament
  of Confirmation.
Be for them light, sanctity, and zeal.

To you, Spirit of truth,
I dedicate my mind, imagination, and
  memory. Enlighten me.
Bring me to fuller knowledge of Jesus
  Christ, and deeper understanding of
  the Gospel and the teaching of the
  Church.
Increase in me the gifts of wisdom,
  knowledge, understanding, and
  counsel.

To you, sanctifying Spirit, I dedicate
my will. Guide me.
Make me faithful in living fully the
commandments and my vocation.
Grant me the gifts of fortitude and
holy fear of God.

To you, life-giving Spirit, I dedicate
my heart. Guard me from evil.
Pour out on me an always greater
abundance of your life.
Bring to completion your work in me.
Grant me the gift of piety. Amen.

Blessed James Alberione

Veni, Sancte Spiritus

Come, Holy Spirit, Creator, come,
from your bright heavenly throne;
come, take possession of our souls,
and make them all your own.

You who are called the Paraclete,
best gift of God above;

the living spring, the living fire,
sweet unction and true love.

You who are sevenfold in your grace,
finger of God's right hand,
his promise, teaching little ones
to speak and understand.

O guide our minds
  with your blest light,
with love our hearts inflame
and with your strength
  which ne'er decays,
confirm our mortal frame.

Far from us drive our hellish foe,
true peace unto us bring;
and through all perils lead us safe
beneath your sacred wing.

Through you may we
  the Father know,
through you, the eternal Son,
and you, the Spirit of them both—
thrice-blessed three in one.

All glory to the Father be,
and to his risen Son,
the like to you, great Paraclete,
while endless ages run. Amen.

Traditonal

Prayer to the Holy Spirit

O Holy Spirit, through the intercession of Mary, Queen of Pentecost:

Heal my mind of lack of reflection,
ignorance, forgetfulness, obstinacy,
prejudice, error, and perversion.
Conceive in me wisdom—Jesus
Christ-Truth in everything.

Heal my heart of indifference, diffi-
dence, bad inclinations, passions,
over sentimentality, and attach-
ments.

Conceive in me good taste, feelings,
 inclinations—Jesus Christ-Life in
 everything.

Heal my will of lack of will power,
 fickleness, inconstancy, sloth, stub-
 bornness, and bad habits.
Conceive in me Jesus Christ-Way in
 everything.

Uplift in a god-like way
intelligence with the gift of understanding,
wisdom with the gift of wisdom,
knowledge with the gift of knowledge,
prudence with the gift of counsel,
justice with the gift of piety,
strength with the gift of spiritual
 strength,
temperance with the gift of fear of
 the Lord.

Blessed James Alberione

Come Holy Spirit

Come, Holy Spirit,
  fill the hearts of your faithful
  and enkindle in them the fire of
    your love.
Send forth your Spirit
  and they shall be created;
  and you shall renew the face of the
    earth.

The Angelus

The Angel of the Lord declared unto
  Mary.
And she conceived of the Holy Spirit.

Hail Mary...

Behold the handmaid of the Lord.
May it be done unto me according to
your word.

Hail Mary...

And the Word became flesh.
And lived among us.

Hail Mary...

V. Pray for us, O Holy Mother of God.
R. That we may be made worthy of
the promises of Christ.

Let us pray. O Lord, it was through
the message of an angel that we learned
of the Incarnation of your Son, Christ.
Pour your grace into our hearts, and
by his passion and cross bring us to the
glory of his resurrection. Through the
same Christ, our Lord. Amen.

Glory be to the Father...

The Rosary

HOW TO PRAY THE ROSARY

The complete Rosary consists of twenty decades, divided into four distinct parts that each contain five decades: the joyful mysteries, which are meditated on Mondays and Saturdays; the luminous mysteries, which are meditated on Thursdays; the sorrowful mysteries, which are meditated on Tuesdays and Fridays; the glorious mysteries, which are meditated on Wednesdays and Sundays.

To pray the Rosary as the blend of contemplative and vocal prayer that it is meant to be, it is recommended to meditate on the individual mysteries while reciting the prayers. In this way, the rosary will bring us closer to Jesus and Mary, and help us grow in our Christian life.

We begin the Rosary by blessing ourselves with the crucifix. Then we may pray the Apostles' Creed, one Our Father, three Hail Marys, and one Glory Be to the Father. Then we pray one Our Father, ten Hail Marys, and one Glory Be to the Father. This completes one decade, and all the other decades are prayed in the same manner with a different mystery meditated during each decade. At the end of the Rosary, the Hail Holy Queen and the Litany of the Blessed Virgin may be prayed.

6.

7.

13.

5.

14.

12.

4.

2.

3.

START
1.

1. Make the Sign of the Cross, and pray the Apostles' Creed.
2. Pray the Our Father.
3. Pray 3 Hail Marys.
4. Pray the Glory. Name the 1st Mystery. Pray the Our Father.
5. Pray 10 Hail Marys.
6. Pray the Glory. Name the 2nd Mystery. Pray the Our Father.
7. Pray 10 Hail Marys.
8. Pray the Glory. Name the 3rd Mystery. Pray the Our Father.
9. Pray 10 Hail Marys.
10. Pray the Glory. Name the 4th Mystery. Pray the Our Father.
11. Pray 10 Hail Marys.
12. Pray the Glory. Name the 5th Mystery. Pray the Our Father.
13. Pray 10 Hail Marys.
14. Pray the Glory and the Hail, Holy Queen.
15. Kiss the crucifix.

8.

9.

10.

11.

FINISH
15.

THE MYSTERIES OF THE ROSARY

Joyful Mysteries (M + Sat)

1. The Annunciation to the Blessed Virgin Mary

2. The Visitation of Mary to Her Cousin Elizabeth

3. The Birth of Jesus at Bethlehem

4. The Presentation of Jesus in the Temple

5. The Finding of Jesus in the Temple

Luminous Mysteries (TH)

1. John Baptizes Jesus in the Jordan

2. Jesus Reveals His Glory at the Wedding of Cana

3. Jesus Proclaims the Kingdom of God and Calls Us to Conversion

4. The Transfiguration of Jesus

5. Jesus Gives Us the Eucharist

Sorrowful Mysteries CT+F

1. Jesus Prays in the Garden of Gethsemane

2. Jesus Is Scourged at the Pillar

3. Jesus Is Crowned with Thorns

4. Jesus Carries the Cross to Calvary

5. Jesus Dies for Our Sins

Glorious Mysteries (W+S)

1. Jesus Rises from the Dead

2. Jesus Ascends into Heaven

3. The Holy Spirit Descends on the Apostles

4. Mary Is Assumed into Heaven

5. Mary Is Crowned Queen of Heaven and Earth

Hail Holy Queen

Hail Holy Queen, Mother of mercy, our life, our sweetness, and our hope! To you we cry, poor banished children of Eve; to you do we send up our sighs, mourning, and weeping in this valley of tears. Turn then, most gracious advocate, your eyes of mercy toward us, and after this our exile, show unto us the blessed fruit your womb, Jesus. O clement, O loving, O sweet Virgin Mary.

The Fatima Prayer

O my Jesus, forgive us our sins, save us from the fires of hell, lead all souls to heaven, especially those most in need of your mercy.

The Litany in Honor of the Most Blessed Virgin Mary

Lord, have mercy.

Christ, have mercy.

Lord, have mercy.

Christ, hear us.

Christ, graciously hear us.

God the Father of Heaven,
   have mercy on us.

God the Son, Redeemer of the world,
   have mercy on us.

God the Holy Spirit,
   have mercy on us.

Holy Trinity, one God,
   have mercy on us.

Holy Mary, pray for us.

Holy mother of God, pray for us.

Holy virgin of virgins, pray for us.

Mother of Christ, pray for us.

Mother of the Church, pray for us.

Mother of divine grace, pray for us.

Mother most pure, pray for us.
Mother most chaste, pray for us.
Mother inviolate, pray for us.
Mother undefiled, pray for us.
Mother most amiable, pray for us.
Mother most admirable, pray for us.
Mother of good counsel, pray for us.
Mother of our Creator, pray for us.
Mother of our Redeemer, pray for us.
Virgin most prudent, pray for us.
Virgin most venerable, pray for us.
Virgin most renowned, pray for us.
Virgin most powerful, pray for us.
Virgin most merciful, pray for us.
Virgin most faithful, pray for us.
Mirror of justice, pray for us.
Seat of wisdom, pray for us.
Cause of our joy, pray for us.
Spiritual vessel, pray for us.
Vessel of honor, pray for us.
Singular vessel of devotion,
  pray for us.

Mystical rose, pray for us.
Tower of David, pray for us.
Tower of ivory, pray for us.
House of gold, pray for us.
Ark of the Covenant, pray for us.
Gate of heaven, pray for us.
Morning star, pray for us.
Health of the sick, pray for us.
Refuge of sinners, pray for us.
Comforter of the afflicted,
  pray for us.
Help of Christians, pray for us.
Queen of angels, pray for us.
Queen of patriarchs, pray for us.
Queen of prophets, pray for us.
Queen of apostles, pray for us.
Queen of martyrs, pray for us.
Queen of confessors, pray for us.
Queen of virgins, pray for us.
Queen of all saints, pray for us.
Queen conceived without original sin,
  pray for us.

Queen assumed into heaven,
  pray for us.
Queen of the most holy Rosary,
  pray for us.
Queen of peace, pray for us.

Lamb of God, who takes away the
  sins of the world, spare us, O Lord.
Lamb of God, who takes away
  the sins of the world,
  graciously hear us, O Lord.
Lamb of God, who takes away the
  sins of the world, have mercy on us.

V. Pray for us, holy Mother of God.
R. That we may be made worthy of
    the promises of Christ.

Let us pray. O God, whose only-begotten Son by his life, death, and resurrection has purchased for us the
rewards of eternal salvation, grant, we
pray, that meditating upon these mys-

teries in the most holy Rosary of the Blessed Virgin Mary, we may imitate what they contain and obtain what they promise. Through Christ our Lord. Amen.

Memorare

Remember, O most gracious Virgin Mary, that never was it known that anyone who fled to your protection, implored your help, or sought your intercession, was left unaided. Inspired with this confidence, I fly to you, O Virgin of virgins, my Mother; to you I come; before you I kneel, sinful and sorrowful. O Mother of the Word Incarnate, despise not my petitions, but hear and answer them. Amen.

Prayer to the
Queen of Apostles

Queen of Apostles, pray for us. Pray for us your children who entrust ourselves entirely to you. Pray for us so that we may never offend Jesus, but may love him with all our hearts. Beneath your mantle, O Mary, we your children take refuge daily. Make us all yours. All that we have is yours. You are our great teacher. Teach us, guide us, and defend us from all danger as you have done until now. And after this our exile, show us Jesus, the blessed fruit of your womb.

Venerable Mother Thecla Merlo

Prayer to Mary

Mary—give us your heart
so beautiful,
so pure,
so immaculate,
your heart so full of love
  and humility,
that we may be able to receive
  and carry Jesus
as you received and carried him
  to others.
You are a cause of joy to us
because you gave us Jesus—
help us to be a cause of joy to others,
  giving only Jesus
to all those with whom
  we come in contact.

Blessed Mother Teresa

Prayer to Mary for Vocations

We turn to you, Mother of the Church. Through your "fiat" you have opened the door, which makes Christ present in the world, in history, and in individual lives. In humble silence and in total availability, you welcomed the call of the Most High. May there be many men and women in our day who respond to your Son's invitation: "Follow me!" Grant them courage to leave family, work, and earthly hopes to follow Christ along the road that he walked. Mary, Queen of Apostles, pray for us and for an increase of priestly and religious vocations. Amen.

Based on a prayer by Pope John Paul II

Angel of God

Angel of God, my guardian dear, to whom God's love entrusts me here, ever this day be at my side to light and guard, to rule and guide. Amen.

To St. Michael the Archangel

St. Michael, the Archangel, defend us in battle. Be our defense against the wickedness and snares of the devil. May God rebuke him, we humbly pray. O prince of the heavenly host, by the power of God cast into hell Satan and the other evil spirits who roam through the world seeking the ruin of souls. Amen.

O Glorious St. Joseph

O glorious St. Joseph, faithful follower of Jesus Christ, to you we raise our hearts and hands to ask your powerful intercession in obtaining from the compassionate heart of Jesus all the helps and graces necessary for our spiritual and temporal welfare, particularly the grace of a happy death, and the special grace for which we now ask *(name it)*.

O guardian of the Word Incarnate, we feel animated with confidence that your prayers for us will be graciously heard at the throne of God.

To St. Paul the Apostle

St. Paul, you traveled the world, never quite knowing where the Spirit would lead you next. You journeyed in faith and accepted beatings, imprisonment, shipwreck, and ultimately martyrdom because of your faith in Jesus Christ.

Help me to accept the great adventure of leading a life faithful to the words of Jesus my Master, the Way, the Truth, and the Life. May I ask myself, "Where does God want me to go today?" On the journey, may I love in the way you taught the Christians of Corinth, and be willing to endure all things for the sake of the Gospel.

Pray with me, that I may heed the voice of the One who called you on the road to Damascus, and set you on the path that leads to life. Amen.

Fr. Jeffrey Mickler, SSP

To St. Jude for Help in Trials

Most holy apostle St. Jude, faithful servant and friend of Jesus, the name of the traitor who delivered your beloved Master into the hands of his enemies has caused you to be forgotten by many. But the Church honors and invokes you universally as the patron of hopeless cases—of things despaired of. Pray for me in my present necessity. Make use, I implore you, of that particular privilege accorded you of bringing visible and speedy help where help is almost despaired of. Come to my assistance in this great need, that I may receive the consolations and help of heaven in all my necessities, tribulations, and sufferings, particularly *(here make your request),* and that I may bless God with you and all the elect throughout eternity.

I promise you, O blessed St. Jude, to be ever mindful of this great favor, and I will never cease to honor you as my special and powerful patron, and to do all in my power to encourage devotion to you. Amen.

Let Love Shine in Us

Lord Jesus,
you know all things,
especially the depth of our hearts.
I plead for our world,
often darkened by hate, envy,
  and rancor.
Let your love and your light
  shine in us
that we might learn how
  to love one another
as brothers and sisters—
children of God, our Father. Amen.

Roberto Mejia Gutierrez

We Have Nowhere
Else to Turn

Heavenly Father, we turn to you in the midst of our tragedy and suffering. We have nowhere else to turn, for you alone are the source of truth and love.

Do not allow us to fall into the pit of bitterness, hatred, and vengeance. Lift us from the depths of our grief and sorrow.

Help us to see that you are always with us, even in the midst of impenetrable darkness. For nothing can separate us from your love.

Keep and watch over us, the sheep of your flock. Amen.

Thomas Dupré

Prayer for the Needs of Others

God of love, whose compassion
   never fails,
we bring you the sufferings
   of the world:
the needs of the homeless,
the cries of prisoners,
the pains of the sick and injured,
the sorrow of the bereaved,
the helplessness of the elderly
   and weak.
According to their needs and
   your great mercy,
strengthen and relieve them
in Jesus Christ our Lord.

St. Anselm

To St. Gerard
for an Expecting Mother

Almighty God, through the work of the Holy Spirit, you prepared the body and soul of the glorious Virgin Mary, Mother of God, to be worthy of your Son. Listen to my prayer through the intercession of St. Gerard, your faithful servant. Protect me/her during pregnancy and childbirth, and safeguard against the evil spirit the tender fruit you have given me/her, in order that, by your saving hand, this child may receive holy Baptism. Grant also that, after living as good Christians on earth, both mother and child may attain everlasting happiness in heaven. Amen.

Prayer for God's Blessing on Medical Personnel

For the wonders of medicine,
  thanks be to God.
For the insight of science,
  thanks be to God.
For doctors and nurses,
  dedication and caring,
  for compassion and competence,
    thanks be to God.
For all hospital workers,
  thanks be to God.
For chaplains and counselors,
  thanks be to God.
For tenderness and thoughtfulness,
  volunteers and social workers,
  for technicians and housekeepers,
    thanks be to God.

Fr. Joe Coleman

Prayer for a Sick Person

Almighty and Eternal God, the everlasting salvation of those who believe, hear me on behalf of *(name)* for whom I implore the aid of your tender mercy, that being restored to bodily health, he/she may give thanks to you in your Church, through Christ our Lord. Amen.

Parents' Prayer

Jesus, only-begotten Son of the Eternal Father, beloved Son of the Blessed Virgin, and foster child of St. Joseph, we fervently implore you, through Mary, your ever Blessed Mother, and your adopted father, St. Joseph, to take our children under your special charge and enclose them in the love of your Sacred Heart. They are the children of your Father in heaven, and they were created after his own image. They are yours, for you have redeemed them with your precious blood. They are temples of the Holy Spirit, who sanctified them in Baptism and implanted in their hearts the virtues of faith, hope, and charity.

O most loving Jesus, rule and guide them, that they may live according to our holy faith, that they may not waver in their confidence in you, and may remain ever faithful in your love. Amen.

Let Me Embrace Others' Pain

Lord, grant me a listening heart
open to your concerns,
open to others' needs.
Give me a large heart
    that embraces all people
of every culture throughout
    the world.

Reconcile people to yourself
    and to one another.
Heal wounds: physical, emotional,
    and spiritual.
Give everyone what is needed
    for survival in this world.

Deepen our awareness
that because you made us for yourself
our hearts will always be restless.

May all of us grow in love for you
    and one another,

so that we may build a new
   earthly city
while we await the eternal city
   of heaven. Amen.

Mary Elizabeth Tebo, FSP

Make the World Better

Hear me, O Lord. I cry to you for help. I ask for the strength to stand strong, for the humility to speak the truth with compassion. Help me to understand the pain that my brother, my sister, my neighbor, my child may be experiencing so that I will be tolerant, helpful, honest, and true.

Grant me the inner love to share my heart and to nurture others. Fill me with your Spirit so that I may walk in faith and make this world a better place, if only for a moment. Amen.

Jaye A. LaVallee

For Protection and Enlightenment

May the strength of God pilot us.
May the power of God preserve us.
May the wisdom of God instruct us.
May the hand of God protect us.
May the way of God direct us.
May the shield of God defend us.
May the hosts of God protect us
  now and always.

St. Patrick

Inspire My Daily Acts of Peace

O God, help me to be a person who radiates your peace. May I show your love to those I live with and rub shoulders with each day,
saying a kind word,
giving in
going out of my way,
being selfless instead of self-centered.

By your grace and power, O God, I believe you can use these small acts to touch hearts in my family, community, country, and world. May your grace multiply goodness and bring peace to all the earth. Amen.

Diane Kraus, FSP

Do It Now, Lord!

At this point in our lives, we turn to you, God our Father.

Your word says, "I will take away your stony hearts and give you hearts of love." This is our need in this hour. Lord, we ask you to do this for us, and to do it now. Reconcile us to one another. Amen.

Livia DeSa

Lord, Make Me an Instrument of Your Peace

Lord, make me an instrument
  of your peace:
where there is hatred, let me sow love;
where there is injury, pardon;
where there is discord, harmony;
where there is error, truth;

where there is doubt, faith;
where there is despair, hope;
where there is darkness, light;
where there is sadness, joy.

Divine Master,
grant that I may not so much seek
to be consoled as to console;
to be understood, as to understand;
to be loved, as to love.

For it is in giving that we receive;
it is in forgetting self
  that we find ourselves;
it is in pardoning
  that we are pardoned;
and it is in dying
  that we are born to eternal life.

St. Francis

A New Prayer for Peace

Lord Jesus, give us an awareness
of the massive forces threatening our
world:

Where there is armed conflict,
let us stretch out our arms to our
brothers and sisters.

Where there is abundance,
let there be simple lifestyles
and sharing.

Where there is poverty,
let there be dignity and constant
striving for justice.

Where there is selfish ambition,
let there be humble service.

Where there is injustice,
let there be atonement.

Where there is despair,
let there be hope in the Good News.

Where there are wounds of division,
let there be unity and wholeness.

Help us to be committed
  to the building of your kingdom:
not seeking to be cared for, but to
  care;
not expecting to be served, but to
  serve others;
not desiring material security, but
  placing our security in your love.

For it is only in loving imitation of
  you, Lord,
that we can discover the healing
  springs of life
to bring about new birth on our earth
and hope for the world. Amen.

Melba Grace Lobaton, FSP

Let Us Be Light

We ask you, merciful Father
that we may treat one another
   with great sensitivity,
always wishing the best
   for each other.

Lord, grant that I may be a bearer
   of light, not of darkness.
Let me always witness to love
   and unity.
May your Spirit show each of us
   the path that leads toward
   an encounter with you. Amen.

Noe Rodriguez

In Our Daily Living

Lord of the world and of peace
help us to unite these two words
in our daily life.

Peace in the world and
  peace in our hearts—
this we ask of you, Lord,
for if there is to be peace in the world,
there must be peace in our hearts.

Remove from us hate and rancor
and everything that impedes
a serene and happy way of life.

Give us your peace, O Lord,
the peace that the world often
does not understand or value,
but without which
the world cannot live.

Gloria Bordeghini, FSP

Praying the Beatitudes

Lord, give me poverty of spirit, so that I always remember that your kingdom is my true home.

Comfort me in my sorrows, Lord. Give me compassion for others who mourn.

Give me a meek heart; empower me to further your kingdom here on earth.

May I hunger and thirst to do your will, Lord; I trust I will find fulfillment only in you.

Lord, give me a merciful heart and surround me with your mercy when I need it most and trust in it least.

Purify my heart, Lord, so that I may see your presence everywhere, and one day see you face to face.

May I bring your peace everywhere I go.

Lord, give me strength, courage,
and perseverance when I am perse-
cuted for doing good.

Grant me a joyful entrance into the
kingdom of heaven.

Marie Paul Curley, FSP

Prayer for Holiness of Life

Godhead! Godhead!
Eternal Godhead!
I proclaim and do not deny it:
you are a peaceful sea
in which the spirit feeds
  and is nourished
while resting in you.
Unite our will with your will
in love's affection and union
so that we will want for nothing
other than becoming holy.

St. Catherine of Siena

Psalm 8

How Majestic Is Your Name

O LORD, our Sovereign,
  how majestic is your name
  in all the earth!
You have set your glory
  above the heavens.
  Out of the mouths of babes
  and infants
you have founded a bulwark
  because of your foes,
  to silence the enemy and the
  avenger.

When I look at your heavens,
  the work of your fingers,
  the moon and the stars that
  you have established;
what are human beings that you
  are mindful of them,
  mortals that you care for them?

Yet you have made them a little
    lower than God,
  and crowned them with glory
    and honor.
You have given them dominion
    over the works of your hands;
  you have put all things under
    their feet,
all sheep and oxen,
  and also the beasts of the field,
the birds of the air, and the fish
    of the sea,
  whatever passes along the paths
    of the seas.

O LORD, our Sovereign,
  how majestic is your name in
    all the earth!

Psalm 146

Praise the Lord!

Praise the LORD!
Praise the LORD, O my soul!
I will praise the LORD as long as I live
  I will sing praises to my God
    all my life long.

Do not put your trust in princes,
  in mortals, in whom there is
    no help.
When their breath departs, they
    return to the earth;
  on that very day their plans perish.

Happy are those whose help is
    the God of Jacob,
  whose hope is in the LORD their God,
who made heaven and earth,
  the sea, and all that is in them;

who keeps faith forever;
  who executes justice for the
    oppressed;
  who gives food to the hungry.

The LORD sets the prisoners free;
  the LORD opens the eyes of the blind.
The LORD lifts up those who are
    bowed down;
  the LORD loves the righteous.
The LORD watches over the strangers;
  he upholds the orphan and
    the widow,
  but the way of the wicked he
    brings to ruin.

The LORD will reign forever,
  your God, O Zion, for all
    generations.
Praise the LORD!

Forgive Me Master

Jesus Master, here I am before your Tabernacle to give an account of my life, of my vocation, of my particular mission.

Infinite Goodness, who with love are patient with my obstinacy, with my continual lack of correspondence, with my deafness, you have conquered me as you conquered Paul. I surrender; always with you, in you, for you.

Forgive me, Master! Don't be silent. I feel like you have brought me to this place of solitude to speak to me, to enlighten me.

Forgive me, Master! Have the same mercy for me as you had with Peter, Magdalene, Matthew, and Thomas.

Deign to receive your prodigal child, who has been unfaithful to your desires.

I wasted all my gifts: my mind, my will, my heart, my time, my energies, my relationships, my health, my blessings, my merits.

All needs to be reconstructed, since I lack the virtue and the faith that you desire. I lack sufficient piety and zeal for God and for souls.

Rebuild in me yourself: I want to leave you free to do with me as you desire. Work in me "until Christ be formed in me," out of these ashes and ruins.

I trust in you, Sacred Heart of the Master.

I trust in you, Immaculate Heart of my Mother.

Blessed James Alberione

Psalm 51

Have Mercy On Me

Have mercy on me, O God,
  according to your steadfast love;
according to your abundant mercy
  blot out my transgressions.
Wash me thoroughly from my
    iniquity,
  and cleanse me from my sin.

For I know my transgressions,
  and my sin is ever before me.
Against you, you alone, have I
    sinned,
  and done what is evil in your sight,
so that you are justified in your
    sentence
  and blameless when you pass
    judgment.

Indeed, I was born guilty,
  a sinner when my mother
    conceived me.

You desire truth in the inward being;
  therefore teach me wisdom in
    my secret heart.
Purge me with hyssop, and I shall
    be clean;
  wash me, and I shall be whiter
    than snow.
Let me hear joy and gladness;
  let the bones that you have
    crushed rejoice.
Hide your face from my sins,
  and blot out all my iniquities.

Create in me a clean heart O God,
  and put a new and right spirit
    within me.

Do not cast me away from your
   presence,
  and do not take your holy spirit
   from me.
Restore to me the joy of your
   salvation,
  and sustain in me a willing spirit.
Then I will teach transgressors
   your ways,
  and sinners will return to you.
Deliver me from bloodshed, O God,
  O God of my salvation,
  and my tongue will sing aloud
   of your deliverance.

O LORD, open my lips,
  and my mouth will declare
   your praise.
For you have no delight in sacrifice;
  if I were to give a burnt offering,
   you would not be pleased.

The sacrifice acceptable to God
   is a broken spirit;
  a broken and contrite heart, O God,
   you will not despise.

Do good to Zion in your good
   pleasure;
  rebuild the walls of Jerusalem,
then you will delight in right
   sacrifices,
  in burnt offerings and whole
   burnt offerings;
  then bulls will be offered on
   your altar.

Lead, Kindly Light

Lead, kindly Light, amid the
  encircling gloom,
Lead thou me on.
The night is dark, and I am far
  from home,
Lead thou me on.
Keep thou my feet; I do not ask to see
The distant scene; one step enough
    for me.

I was not ever thus,
  nor prayed that thou
Should lead me on.
I loved to choose and see my path;
  but now
Lead thou me on.
I loved the garish day,
  and, spite of fears,
Pride ruled my will: remember not
  past years.

So long thy power has blest me,
  sure it still
Will lead me on
O'er moor and fen, o'er crag
  and torrent, till
The night is gone,
And with the morn,
  those angel faces smile
While I have loved long since,
  and lost awhile.

John Henry Newman

An Act of Contrition

O my God, I am heartily sorry for having offended you, and I detest all my sins, because of your just punishments, but most of all because they offend you, my God, who are all good and deserving of all my love. I firmly resolve, with the help of your grace, to sin no more and to avoid the near occasions of sin.

Psalm 25
(vv 4–7)

Be Mindful of Your Mercy

Make me to know your ways, O Lord;
  teach me your paths.
Lead me in your truth, and teach me,
  for you are the God of my salvation;
  for you I wait all day long.

Be mindful of your mercy, O Lord,
    and of your steadfast love,
  for they have been from of old.
Do not remember the sins of my
    youth or my transgressions;
  according to your steadfast love
    remember me
  for our goodness' sake, O Lord!

The Mercy of God

Most Merciful Jesus, whose very nature it is to have compassion on us and to forgive us, do not look upon our sins, but upon the trust which we place in Your infinite goodness. Receive us all into the abode of Your most compassionate heart, and never let us escape from it. We beg this of You by Your love, which unites You to the Father and the Holy Spirit.

Eternal Father, turn Your merciful gaze upon all mankind and especially upon poor sinners, all enfolded in the most compassionate heart of Jesus. For the sake of his sorrowful passion, show us Your mercy that we may praise the omnipotence of Your mercy for ever and ever. Amen.

St. Faustina Kowalska

Prayer of Surrender

Father,
I abandon myself into your hands;
do with me what you will.
Whatever you may do, I thank you;
I am ready for all, I accept all.
Let only your will be done in me,
and in all your creatures.

I wish no more than this, O Lord.

Into your hands I commend myself;
I offer myself to you with all the love
of my heart,
for I love you, Lord,
and so need to give myself,
to surrender myself into you hands
without reserve,
and with boundless confidence
because you are my Father.

Blessed Charles de Foucauld

Help Me Trust in Darkness

Thank you, Lord, for everything—for my life and those you have given to me. Please keep everyone I love safe!

Lord, help me to recognize you in all the "disguises" you wear, so that I never fail to feed the hungry, comfort the ill, visit the prisoners. I know I was sent here to be a blazing spark of your love, to help you in your ever-continuing expression of creation. Keep my eyes and heart open so that I never fail to gasp at the wonder and beauty of your creation.

I want to always trust you, even when I don't understand why you sometimes seem to have disappeared. Help me in dark times to remember that the other side of the cross is rebirth. I trust you in everything. Amen.

Antoinette Bosco

Litany for the Journey Home

Deliverer, deliver me.
Liberator, set me free.
Word Incarnate, whisper care.
Way of Truth, lead me there.
Prince of Peace, calm my fears.
Consolation, dry my tears.
Savior of all, save.
Swing wide, Gate.
Light from light, illuminate.
Helper, healer, make me whole.
Bread of Life, fill my soul.
Vindicator, forgive my sin.
Shepherd of souls, gather me in.
Son of David,
King of kings,
Be the hymn my heartbeat sings.
Living water, wash me in calm,
...drown me in joy,
...carry me home.
Carry me home. Amen.

Fr. Joe Coleman

Prayer for Strength in Letting a Loved One Go

I must let go *(Lord, help me let go...)*
not of the memories,
not of the love.

I will let go *(Lord, help me let go...)*
that his/her light may return
  to the Light.
I will release this hand that I hold,
I will stop taking that suffering face
  into my hands,
I will give over to you what is yours.

(Lord, please help me let go.)
That he/she may go to you,
  I will let go.

Lord help me let go...
that he/she may rest in you...
that he/she may know your peace.

Lord, help me let go.

Fr. Joe Coleman

Psalm 130

Out of the Depths

Out of the depths I cry to you,
   O Lord.
  Lord, hear my voice!
Let your ears be attentive
  to the voice of my supplication!

If you, O Lord, should mark
   iniquities,
  Lord, who could stand?
But there is forgiveness with you,
  so that you may be revered.

I wait for the Lord, my soul waits,
  and in his word I hope;
my soul waits for the Lord
  more than those who watch
   for the morning,
  more than those who watch
   for the morning.

O Israel, hope in the LORD!
  For with the LORD there is
    steadfast love
  and with him is great power to
    redeem.
It is he who will redeem Israel
  from all its iniquities.

To St. Joseph for the Dying

St. Joseph, foster father of our Lord Jesus Christ, and true spouse of the Virgin Mary, pray for us and for the dying of this day.

Eternal Rest

Eternal rest grant to them, O Lord, and let perpetual light shine upon them. May they rest in peace. Amen.

Sacrament of the Anointing of the Sick

We should call a priest when someone begins to be in danger of death from sickness, accident, or old age so that he or she may receive grace and consolation from the Sacrament of Anointing of the Sick. Christ's minister should be called to visit the sick in any serious illness even when death does not seem near, because he will bring them the sacraments they need.

Those who are in danger of death should be told of their condition so that they may prepare themselves to receive Christ in the sacraments. It is recommended to call a priest before a person loses consciousness.

In case of sudden or unexpected death, always call a priest, because absolution and the anointing can be given conditionally for some time after apparent death.

The elderly who are in a weakened condition are also encouraged by the Church to receive the Anointing of the Sick, even though no dangerous illness is present.

Rite of Holy Communion outside Mass

Communion in Ordinary Circumstances

INTRODUCTORY RITES

Greeting

The minister greets the sick person and the others present.

The peace of the Lord be with you always.
And also with you.

Other greetings may be used.

The minister then places the Blessed Sacrament on the table, and all join in adoration.

Sprinkling with Holy Water

If it seems desirable, the priest or deacon may sprinkle the sick person and those present with holy water.

If the Sacrament of Penance is now celebrated, the penitential rite is omitted.

PENITENTIAL RITE

The minister invites the sick person and all present to join in the penitential rite.

After a brief period of silence, the penitential rite continues, using one of the following:

A

Lord Jesus, you healed the sick:
Lord, have mercy.
Lord, have mercy.

Lord Jesus, you forgave sinners:
Christ, have mercy.
Christ, have mercy.

Lord Jesus, you give us yourself
to heal us and bring strength:
Lord, have mercy.
Lord, have mercy.

B

All say:

I confess to almighty God, and to you, my brothers and sisters, that I have sinned through my own fault

They strke their breast.

in my thoughts and in my words, in what I have done, and in what I have failed to do; and I ask blessed Mary, ever virgin, all the angels and saints, and you, my brothers and sisters, to pray for me to the Lord our God.

The minister concludes the penitential rite with the following:

May almighty God have mercy on us, forgive us our sins,

and bring us to everlasting life.

Amen.

LITURGY OF THE WORD

Reading

The word of God is proclaimed by one of those present or by the minister.

Response

A brief period of silence may be observed after the reading of the word of God.

The minister may then give a brief explanation of the reading, applying it to the needs of the

sick person and those who are looking after
him or her.

General Intercessions

The general intercessions may be said. With a
brief introduction the minister invites all those
present to pray. After the intentions the minister says the concluding prayer. It is desirable
that the intentions be announced by someone
other than the minister.

Liturgy of Holy Communion

The Lord's Prayer

The minister introduces the Lord's Prayer

All say:

Our Father...

Communion

The minister shows the Eucharistic bread to
those present.

The sick person and all who are to receive
communion say:

**Lord, I am not worthy to receive
you, but only say the word and I shall
be healed.**

The minister goes to the sick person and, showing the Blessed Sacrament says:

The body of Christ.

The sick person answers: "Amen," and receives communion.

Then the minister says:

The blood of Christ.

The sick person answers: "Amen," and receives communion.

Others present who wish to receive communion then do so in the usual way.

After the conclusion of the rite, the minister cleanses the vessel as usual.

Silent Prayer

Then a period of silence may be observed.

Prayer after Communion

The minister says a concluding prayer.

CONCLUDING RITE

Blessing

Communion in a Hospital or Institution

INTRODUCTORY RITES

Antiphon

The rite may begin in the church, the hospital chapel, or the first room, where the minister says an antiphon.

If it is customary, the minister may be accompanied by a person carrying a candle.

LITURGY OF HOLY COMMUNION

Greeting

On entering each room, the minister may use the following greeting:

**The peace of the Lord
be with you always.
And also with you.**

The minister then places the Blessed Sacrament on the table, and all join in adoration.

If there is time and it seems desirable, the minister may proclaim a Scripture reading.

The Lord's Prayer

When circumstances permit (for example, when there are not many rooms to visit), the minister is encouraged to lead the sick in the Lord's Prayer. The minister introduces the Lord's Prayer.

All say:

Our Father...

Communion

The minister shows the Eucharistic bread to those present.

The sick person and all who are to receive communion say:

Lord, I am not worthy to receive you, but only say the word and I shall be healed.

The minister goes to the sick person and, showing the Blessed Sacrament says:

The body of Christ.

The sick person answers: "Amen," and receives communion.

Then the minister says:

The blood of Christ.

The sick person answers: "Amen," and receives communion.

Others present who wish to receive communion then do so in the usual way.

CONCLUDING RITE

Concluding Prayer

The concluding prayer may be said either in the last room visited, in the church, or chapel.

Acknowledgments

The Sign of the Cross, p. 9; The Lord's Prayer, p. 9; Hail Mary, p. 9; Glory Be, p. 10; Morning Offering, p. 10; An Act of Faith, p. 11; An Act of Hope, p. 12; An Act of Love, p. 12; The Apostles' Creed, p. 14; Prayer Before a Crucifix, p. 25; The Angelus, p. 46; The Rosary, p. 48; Hail Holy Queen, p. 54; Memorare, p. 59; Angel of God, p. 63; An Act of Contrition, p. 97; Eternal Rest, p. 105; Sacrament of the Anointing of the Sick, p. 106:

From Basic Prayers. *Copyright © 1983, Daughters of St. Paul. Published by Pauline Books & Media. All Rights Reserved.*

An Evening Prayer, p. 10; Stations of the Cross, p. 26; Soul of Christ, p. 33:

From Queen of Apostles Prayerbook, *compiled by the Daughters of Saint Paul. Copyright © 1991, Daughters of St. Paul. Published by Pauline Books & Media. All Rights Reserved.*

Prayer for the Gift of Sleep, p. 14; Prayer for God's Blessing on Medical Personnel, p. 71; Litany for the Journey Home, p. 102; Prayer for Strength in Letting a Loved One Go, p. 103:

When We Most Need You, p. 15; Let Love Shine in Us, p. 67; We Have Nowhere Else to Turn, p. 68; Let Me Embrace Others' Pain, p. 74; Make the World Better, p. 75; Inspire My Daily Acts of Peace, p. 77; Do It Now, Lord!, p. 78; A New Prayer for Peace, p. 80; Let Us Be Light, p. 82; In Our Daily Living, p. 83; Help Me Trust in Darkness, p. 101:

Prayer of Trust in Darkness, p. 16; Prayer of Longing for Christ, p. 23; Hymn to Christ, p. 24; Prayer for the Needs of Others, p. 69; For Protection and Enlightenment, p. 76; Prayer for Holiness of Life, p. 85; Lead, Kindly Light, p. 96; Prayer of Surrender, p. 100:

Let Nothing Disturb Thee, p. 18:

Too Late Have I Loved You, p. 18:

In Thanksgiving, p. 31; The Mercy of God, p. 99:

Come Holy Spirit, p. 46:

Alphabetical Index of Prayers

A

C

R

S

BOOKS & MEDIA

The Daughters of St. Paul operate book and media centers at the following addresses. Visit, call or write the one nearest you today, or find us on the World Wide Web, www.pauline.org

CALIFORNIA

3908 Sepulveda Blvd, Culver City,
 CA 90230   310-397-8676

5945 Balboa Avenue, San Diego,
 CA 92111   858-565-9181

46 Geary Street, San Francisco,
 CA 94108   415-781-5180

FLORIDA

145 SW 107th Avenue, Miami,
 FL 33174   305-559-6715

HAWAII

1143 Bishop Street, Honolulu,
 HI 96813   808-521-2731
Neighbor Islands call: 800-259-8463

ILLINOIS

172 North Michigan Avenue,
 Chicago, IL 60601
 312-346-4228

LOUISIANA

4403 Veterans Memorial Blvd,
 Metairie, LA 70006   504-887-7631

MASSACHUSETTS

885 Providence Hwy, Dedham,
 MA 02026   781-326-5385

MISSOURI

9804 Watson Road, St. Louis,
 MO 63126   314-965-3512

NEW JERSEY

561 U.S. Route 1, Wick Plaza, Edison,
 NJ 08817   732-572-1200

NEW YORK

150 East 52nd Street, New York,
 NY 10022   212-754-1110

78 Fort Place, Staten Island, NY
 10301   718-447-5071

PENNSYLVANIA

9171-A Roosevelt Blvd, Philadelphia,
 PA 19114   215-676-9494

SOUTH CAROLINA

243 King Street, Charleston, SC
 29401   843-577-0175

TENNESSEE

4811 Poplar Avenue, Memphis,
 TN 38117   901-761-2987

TEXAS

114 Main Plaza, San Antonio, TX
 78205   210-224-8101

VIRGINIA

1025 King Street, Alexandria, VA
 22314   703-549-3806

CANADA

3022 Dufferin Street, Toronto, Ontario,
 Canada M6B 3T5   416-781-9131

1155 Yonge Street, Toronto, Ontario,
 Canada M4T 1W2   416-934-3440

¡También somos su fuente para libros, videos y música en español!